AMERICAN
FOOTBALL
RULES IN PICTURES

AMERICAN FOOTBALL

RULES IN PICTURES

Edited by Don Schiffer and Lud Duroska
Foreword by Mel Hein,

SUPERVISOR OF OFFICIALS,

AMERICAN FOOTBALL CONFERENCE

Introduction by Clary Anderson

HEAD FOOTBALL COACH,

MONTCLAIR STATE COLLEGE

Illustrated by George Kraynak

COLUMBUS BOOKS
LONDON

First published in Great Britain in 1986 by
Columbus Books
19-23 Ludgate Hill, London EC4M 7JP

The authors wish to express their appreciation
of the help given so generously by the National Collegiate
Athletic Association; the National Federation of
State High School Athletic Associations; the National Football
League, Jim Hefferman, Jack Horrigan and Mel Hein;
and Steve Gerdy.

Printed and bound by
The Guernsey Press, Guernsey, Channel Islands

ISBN 0 86287 141 7

A GREAT SPORT

Football, on the field and off, has been the dominant factor in my life. It has taught me discipline and team play . . . it has taught me that there are winners and losers, and that winners don't always keep winning, nor do losers always keep losing.

I can think of no better training for a productive life than competition in football on the high school, college and professional levels. The sport demands desire and ability to take the initiative. Strength is necessary but so is courage. Characteristics like these are most necessary if a man is to lead a productive and meaningful life for himself and his family.

Persons in the stands profit from football, too, and this goes beyond those few hours of entertainment. They are made aware of the necessity of a man's combining his top physical and mental qualities for ultimate success. Brought home, too, as they watch the flow of action which has been described as everything from a master chess game to a "war without casualties" is the realization that, all things being equal, eleven men attuned to each other and aware of the other man's position must ultimately come out ahead of eleven individualists.

Mel Hein, All-America at Washington State, starred for fifteen years, 1931–45, as center and linebacker (those were pre-two-platoon days) for the New York Giants. In 1938 he was voted the Most Valuable Player in the National Football League, the only interior lineman to be so honored. He is a member of both the College and Pro Football Halls of Fame, and was a charter member of the Pro Football Hall of Fame.

CONTENTS

THE IMPORTANCE OF KNOWING THE RULES

In the courtroom a Judge often has to tell an offender that "Ignorance of the Law is no excuse." How true in sports!

I doubt that there is a coach who doesn't remember a game that was lost because a player didn't know a rule and committed a violation. The player's intentions may have been thoroughly honest, but the officials have to go by the "law" — the rules of the game — and the needless penalty determined the outcome of the contest.

That is one of the reasons why a book such as this one, devoted as it is to interpreting and clarifying the fundamental rules of football, is an important aid to the player who is learning the game. Through the illustrations and the explanations, he learns what can and what cannot be done. The devise of having offensive players in white jerseys and the defensive players in black helps make the action easier to follow.

The more thoroughly a player learns the rules right from the start, the better equipped he is as a competitor, and the less likely he is to make mistakes. And mistakes cost ballgames.

But this book is not only for the player. It is also for the football fan. By becoming more familiar with the rules and particularly with the official's signals, the spectator in the stands and the spectator at home before his TV screen can better understand what is going on and why. The spectator's enjoyment of the game increases with his knowledge.

Rules were created and are enforced to insure fair play for both teams. Football wouldn't be a sport without them — it's essential that we know the rules and use them properly.

CLARY ANDERSON

Clary Anderson, presently the head football coach at Montclair State College, has been a successful coach for nearly four decades on both the high school and college levels. He has compiled one of the outstanding records in the country, having won more than 90 per cent of his games. He is the author of *Make the Team in Football*.

RULE DIFFERENCES

The rules illustrated and interpreted in this book are fundamental and apply equally to high school, college, and professional football except where noted otherwise. In extracting the essential meaning and purpose of the key rules, the editors relied on a variety of codes, including those used by the National Collegiate Athletic Association, the National Federation of State High School Athletic Associations, and the National Football League.

In contrast to baseball, where the rules are virtually the same regardless of the level at which the sport is played, football has never achieved uniformity. The primary reasons for this are that football is a more rugged game with much greater physical contact and that football strategy and tactics are more complex. This is particularly true of the professional sport, whose players are more mature and possess greater physical skill, and whose officials are more mindful of putting on games that continue to be exciting and appeal to the general public. This combination accounts for football's changing nature.

The most recent example of a sweeping change in the rules occurred on April 25, 1974 when the NFL adopted a sudden-death overtime period for all its games, moved the goal posts back to the end line, and made other changes to "open up" the passing attack and aid kickoff and punt returns.

Unlike high schools and colleges, which have never had an overtime rule, the professionals have had one since 1947 but solely for their playoff and championship games. The purpose in extending this rule to all pre-season and regular-season games, of course, is to reduce the number of tie results. The NFL decided to add one tie-break period of 15 minutes to each tie game. The team that scores first, whether by safety, field goal, or touchdown, wins. If neither team scores during the period, the game then ends officially as a tie. (In the playoffs and the Super Bowl, the teams will continue to play as many overtime periods as necessary until a score is made to break the tie.)

By positioning the goal posts 10 yards back from the goal line, to the end line of the end zone, the NFL reversed a rule that had been on the books for 41 years. The pros' thinking in 1933 was that moving the goal posts up to the goal line would increase the opportunities to score field goals. And it certainly did! In the last decade especially, as the kicking specialists became ever more proficient, the numerous field goals cheapened the value of the touchdown. (Incidentally, the college authorities, who originally had the goal posts on the goal line, moved them back in 1927 to the end line, where they have remained ever since. The reason for their move was concern for the players' safety. It was more unlikely that players would collide with the posts at the end line position.)

The NFL, however, is retaining the length of the crossbar between the uprights at 18 feet 6 inches while the colleges will still use a crossbar nearly 5 feet longer, with uprights 23 feet 4 inches apart.

The NFL also decided that the field-goal attempt should be made more of a gamble by requiring that the ball be returned to the line of scrimmage or the 20-yard line, whichever is farther from the goal line, in the event of a missed kick. Previously, it cost a team nothing to try for a long field goal instead of punting because if the 3-point attempt missed, the opposing team took possession on its own 20-yard line. With the new ruling, a team will think twice before attempting a long field goal and risk turning the ball over to their opponents in favorable field position.

Passing, notably the long touchdown "bombs," had been made more difficult in recent seasons by the harassing and "bumping" tactics of the defenders against the receivers. To counter this somewhat, the NFL determined that a receiver cannot be knocked out of a play by a block below the waist—the "roll" or cross-body block—and once he is 3 yards past the line of scrimmage, he can be hit or "bumped" only once by a defensive player. The penalty for holding by an offensive player, common in pass-blocking situations, was lessened from 15 yards to 10 yards.

To promote more and longer kickoff returns, the NFL pushed the kickoff line back from the kicking team's 40-yard line to the 35, while punt returns are encouraged by the new rule that players on the kicking team cannot cross the line of scrimmage until the ball is kicked.

Through the years an important source of difference has been the sub-stitution rule, with the pros proving more consistent in this respect than the collegians. After employing the free-substitution rule from 1943 to 1945 because of wartime conditions, the pros adopted the rule—popularly known as the two-platoon rule—permanently in 1950. It allows the teams to sub-stitute without restriction at any time except when the ball is actually in play.

Many observers credit the increasing popularity of professional football to this rule. It has made possible the use of offensive and defensive platoons, enabling players to concentrate their skills on the phase of the game in which they excel. Teams can also compete at full speed since each platoon can rest on the bench when the other platoon is in action. The art of specialization has been refined to such an extent that special platoons go in for specific action, such as the kick-off or the punt.

Another difference in the rules is scoring the try-for-point after a touch-down. In an attempt to reduce the number of tie games, colleges adopted a two-point rule. If the ball is carried or passed successfully over the goal line — in the same manner as scoring a touchdown — the try counts for 2 points. If the team elects to place-kick (convert) the try, then it is worth only 1 point.

Most high schools follow the college rule while the other schools and the National Football League have continued with the old rule crediting only 1 point whether the successful try is a kick, run or pass.

The colleges also spot the ball for the try after touchdown on the 3-yard line while high schools and the professionals spot the ball on the 2-yard line.

On running plays, the colleges and high schools differ from the pros as to whether the runner may continue after he slips or falls to the ground without being tackled. The professionals permit the runner to continue — even though his knee, for example, may have touched the ground — so long as contact has not been made by a defensive player. The runner may not advance, under college and high school rules, after any part of his body except his hands and feet touches the ground.

A last basic difference concerns the recovery of fumbles. All three sets of rules permit any player from either team to advance with a fumble if the ball is caught in the air. When the fumble has touched the ground, the college rule states that only the team that has fumbled can advance the ball. The opposing team can only recover it. Under professional and high school rules a fumble may be picked up and advanced by any player on either team.

DEFINITIONS OF TERMS

Batting: Striking the ball intentionally with a hand or arm. It is permissible for any player eligible to touch a forward pass to bat the ball while the pass is in the air. It is also permissible to bat the ball if the player is blocking a punt. In other cases of a free ball, batting is illegal. The penalty is 15 yards.

Blocker: A player using his body to obstruct an opponent. An offensive blocker must observe the restrictions on the use of hands and arms.

Clipping: A type of block in which the player runs or dives into the back or the back of the legs of an opponent other than the runner. Clipping is legal in line play if it done in a rectangular area which is 4 yards wide on each side of the middle offensive lineman and 3 yards deep on either side of the scrimmage line. In the open field clipping is illegal. The penalty is 15 yards from the spot of the foul.

Crawling: An attempt by the runner to advance the ball after he has been tackled. The penalty is 5 yards.

Delay of Game: Any failure by a team to be ready for play within the specified time limit or any action that prolongs the game. The penalty is 5 yards.

Double Foul: When both teams commit fouls and the penalties offset each other.

Down: The unit of play. When a team has first down, it has four plays, or downs, in which to gain 10 yards to retain possession of the ball. If the first down is within the opponent's 10-yard line, then the team has four downs to gain the remaining distance to the goal line.

Fair Catch: A receiver of a kick signals for a fair catch by raising one arm directly above his head. He then is protected against being tackled when he makes the catch but gives up his right to advance the ball.

Field Goal: The ball is place-kicked or drop-kicked from scrimmage over the opposing team's crossbar. The kick scores 3 points.

Forward Pass: A pass thrown on a scrimmage play toward the opponent's goal line. Only the offensive team may throw a forward pass, and it must be thrown in or behind the neutral zone.

Foul: Any infraction of the rules that will draw a penalty.

Free Ball: A live ball in play, except for a forward pass, that is not in possession of a player.

Fumble: When a player loses possession of the ball, except when he passes, kicks or hands the ball off.

Goal Line: The line that has to be reached or crossed by the team in possession of the ball in order to score a touchdown. The goal lines separate the end zones from the 100-yard field of play.

Half: The game is divided into two halves, each half is divided into two periods, or quarters. The half is started with a kick-off. Playing time of a half is 30 minutes in College and Professional football, 24 minutes in High School. Teams may leave the field at the end of the first half. Halftime intermission is 15 minutes in High School and College games, 20 minutes in Professional football.

Huddle: Players get together in a group, usually forming a circle, to decide on the strategy and the signals for the next play. The huddle is not limited to the offensive team. The defensive team may also huddle to determine what strategy to follow.

Hurdling: The runner jumps over or attempts to jump over a player who is on his feet in the open field. At the scrimmage line, hurdling is defined as jumping over a player with both feet or both knees foremost. It is illegal and the penalty is 15 yards.

Interception: The catching of any pass by an opponent who is then allowed to run with the ball.

Kicking: a) Drop-kick: The kicker drops the ball and kicks it just as it touches or rises from the ground.
  b) Kick-off: The ball is put into play by a place-kick, drop-kick, or with the use of a tee, at the start of the game, the start of the second half, after a field goal or try-for-point after a touchdown. The kick-off takes place from the 40-yard line of the kicking team.
  c) Place-kick: The ball is held for the kicker by a teammate.
  d) Punt: The ball is kicked before it touches the ground on a scrimmage play or as a free kick after a safety is scored.
  e) Return-kick: A kick made by a player immediately after catching a kick; it is now seldom used.

Lateral: This is also known as a backward pass. Any player may pass the ball backward or parallel to his goal line to a teammate at any time.

Line-to-gain: The yard line 10 yards in advance of the most forward point of the ball that the team must reach in four downs or lose possession of the ball.

Man-in-motion: One player of the offensive backfield may be in motion before and as the ball is snapped, but he must be moving away from or parallel to the defensive team's goal line. In high school, if the back starts from the scrimmage line, he must stop for one second before going in motion and must be 5 yards in back of the line when the ball is snapped. The pro rule requires the man in motion to start at least 1 yard in back of the scrimmage line. If he is illegally in motion, the penalty is 5 yards.

9

Multiple Foul: When two or more fouls are committed by a team, the opposing team has a choice of penalties.

Neutral Zone: An area the length of the football that is between the offensive and defensive scrimmage lines.

Offside: When any part of the player's body is beyond his scrimmage line, or his restraining line before the ball is in play.

Out-of-bounds: The area outside the sidelines and endlines including the lines. The ball or a player touching the sideline or endline is considered out-of-bounds.

Period: The total time of the game is divided into four quarters, or periods. In College and Professional football each period lasts 15 minutes; in High School games it is 12 minutes long. Two periods make a half. Play in the first and third period begins with a kick-off. The second and fourth periods start after an exchange of goals, but play is resumed from the point where it was stopped by the end of the previous period. Before the second and fourth periods there is an intermission of one or two minutes, but players are not permitted to leave the field.

Recovering: Gaining possession of the ball after a fumble.

Runner: Player who is in possession of the ball.

Safety: Two points scored by the team not in possession of the ball. Among the ways a safety is scored are: the runner is tackled in his end zone or goes out-of-bounds from the end zone; the offensive team fumbles the ball out-of-bounds from the end zone; the snap from center goes out of the end zone, and the defensive team is responsible for the ball becoming dead in the offensive team's end zone, with the ball still in possession of the offensive team.

Scrimmage: The action that results when a play starts with the center snapping the ball back and ends when the ball is dead.

Scrimmage Line: The imaginary line established for each team by the point of the ball nearest its goal line. The offensive team must have at least 7 players on or within a foot of the scrimmage line. Defensive players may be positioned anywhere behind their scrimmage line.

Shift: When two or more players of the offensive team change position after lining up and before the ball is snapped. After a shift, all offensive players must remain stationary for a second before the snap.

Snap: When the center passes or hands the ball back to a backfield player. Also known as centering the ball.

Tackle: The maneuver by which a defensive player stops the runner by using his hands, arms or body.

Time-out: When play is stopped at the request of either team for a period of 1½ minutes. The time-out may be of longer duration when necessary, such as when medical attention is given to an injured player. The referee also may call timeouts at his discretion.

Touchback: When the offensive team is responsible for putting the ball in the defensive team's end zone while giving up possession of the ball on such plays as the kick-off or punt. After a touchback, the team with the ball starts the next play with a first down on its 20-yard-line.

Touchdown: Six points are scored when a player in possession of the ball reaches the goal line or is in the end zone of the opposing team by running, catching a pass or recovering a fumble.

Try-for-point: The play that follows a touchdown even if time has run out in a period. The team scoring the touchdown has one play from scrimmage in which to run or pass the ball over the goal line or to place or drop-kick the ball over the crossbar. In High School, College and Professional play, a successful kick scores 1 point. In College and most High School games, a successful run or pass scores 2 points. In the National Football League and some High School games, a successful run or pass scores 1 point.

DIAGRAM OF FIELD

THE FIELD

The playing field is 360 feet long and 160 feet wide. When the dimensions are given in yards, the rectangular field is 120 yards long by 53⅓ yards wide. The *goal lines* are 300 feet (100 yards) apart. At each end of the field there is an *end zone*, 30 feet (10 yards) deep. The goal lines, which are located within the end zones, and the end zones are the area in which touchdowns and safeties are scored.

The field is marked every 5 yards by a distinct line running across the width of the field from sideline to sideline.

The entire playing field is bordered by a solid line. The area within the sidelines and the endlines is *inbounds*. The sidelines and the endlines themselves, as well as the area beyond these lines, are *out-of-bounds*.

On the field, parallel to the sidelines and running from goal line to goal line, are two *inbounds lines*. These divide the field into three equal parts, each 53 feet, 4 inches wide. In Professional football the inbounds lines are 70 feet 9 inches from the sidelines. When a play ends out-of-bounds or in a *side zone* (between the sideline and the inbounds line), the ball is placed at the nearer inbounds line for the next play.

The teams have a place on opposite sides of the field for a players' bench, coaches and other authorized personnel. These are called *team areas* and are located between the 35-yard lines. They are 5 to 6 feet from the sidelines.

Flags with flexible staffs are placed at each corner formed by the goal line and a sideline.

YARDAGE CHAIN AND DOWN MARKER

The *yardage chain* is exactly 10 yards long when fully extended. It is joined to two rods, each at least 5 feet high. It is used to measure if the offensive team has *gained* at least *10 yards* in *four downs* (plays) or less. When at least 10 yards has been gained, the offensive team has made a *first down* and has four downs again in which to gain another 10 yards.

The *down indicator* is on a rod that is at least 4 feet high and holds four "cards" lettered 1, 2, 3 and 4. The indicator marks the most forward point of the ball at the *start of each down* and the "card" indicating the number of the down is displayed.

THE GOAL POSTS

The *goal posts* are located on the end lines. The posts are 18 feet, 6 inches apart in both High School and Professional football. Posts in College games are placed 23 feet, 4 inches apart. In all cases, the *crossbar* is placed 10 feet above the ground. Professional rules require that the goal posts must be *padded* with kapok or foam rubber. "Offset" posts, set behind the end line but with the crossbar extended to the end line, are used in Professional football.

SCHOOL

PROFESSIONAL

Under College rules, no markings may be placed in the end zones that are closer than 2 feet to the goal line, the endlines or the sidelines.

THE FOOTBALL

The football must weigh between 14 and 15 ounces. It is to be inflated to an air pressure of between 12½ and 13½ pounds. The *long circumference* must measure between 28 and 28½ inches. The *short circumference* must be between 21¼ and 21½ inches.

In High School games, the football used, either rubber- or leather-covered, should be of a natural tan color with white 1-inch stripes, 3 to 3½ inches from each end of the football to the near edge of the stripe. Another color may be used with the approval of both teams.

In College games, the football should be of a natural tan color, but a white or colored ball, with or without stripes, may be used for night games.

In Professional games, the football is to be of a natural tan color for day games and of a brown color with white stripes for night games.

STANDARD NUMBERING SYSTEM

To help identify players by position, a *standard numbering system* is *recommended* for High Schools and Colleges. The numbers assigned for *ends* are 80 to 89; for *tackles,* 70 to 79; for *guards,* 60 to 69; for *centers,* 50 to 59; and for *backs,* 1 to 49.

While this numbering system is only *recommended* for High Schools and Colleges, Professional football has *required* standard numbering for many years. Starting with the 1973 season, NFL players are numbered as follows: *quarterbacks* and *kickers,* 1 to 19; all *running* and *defensive backs,* 20 to 49; *centers* and *linebackers,* 50 to 59; *defensive linemen* and *interior offensive linemen* (except for *centers*), 60 to 79, and *wide receivers* and *tight ends,* 80 to 89. (All players who were in the NFL prior to 1973 may use their old numbers.)

Regardless of his number, however, a player may play any position; in some cases the referee must be notified of the change of position.

IMPROPER EQUIPMENT

A player will be ordered off the field by the official for an improper uniform. In this case, the number on the player's jersey is too small. *Numbers* must be at least *8 inches* high on the front of the jersey, and *10 inches* on the back.

This player will be ordered off the field and not allowed in the game until he has changed his jersey. Any equipment which, in the opinion of the officials, would confuse the opposing players is illegal.

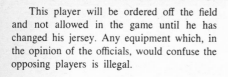

Jerseys or helmets that are similar in color the football and tend to conceal it are for- den. The use of camouflage of any sort is gal and players will not be permitted on field until the infraction of the rules is rected.

This player, too, will be ordered off the field because he is too well protected. Players are not permitted to have leather, or other hard material, regardless of how well it is covered or padded, on hands, wrists, forearms or elbows.

Backfield stars have been described as being "slippery as an eel," but any material that helps them achieve such elusiveness is strictly forbidden. The use of oil, grease or any slippery substance on the player's uniform is illegal.

A player will not be allowed in the game if he wears a face mask with sharp edges. Face masks should be of non-breakable, molded plastic with rounded edges or with rubber-covered wire.

THE REFEREE

The *referee* has over-all charge and control of the game. His decisions are final except in those matters specifically under the jurisdiction of other officials. Among his duties are spotting the ball where play is to resume, declaring the ball in play or dead, signalling infractions of rules and pacing off the penalties. He is the authority for the score.

THE UMPIRE

The *umpire* has primary jurisdiction over the equipment and the conduct of the players. In each scrimmage he is particularly responsible for observing illegal play. He must also cover open play that develops after the linemen make their initial charge.

THE LINESMAN

The *linesman* has primary jurisdiction over the neutral zone and infractions (called OFFSIDE) of the scrimmage formation. Under the supervision of the referee, he marks the progress of the ball and keeps an accurate count of the downs. Under his direction assistants operate the yardage chain to mark and hold the starting point and *line-to-gain* for each series of downs as well as the *down indicator*.

THE LINE JUDGE

The *line judge* keeps time of game as a backup for the clock operator, and checks for offside, encroachment and other actions pertaining to the scrimmage line prior to or at the snap.

THE FIELD JUDGE

The *field judge*, when there is no Back Judge, has primary jurisdiction over the timing of the game. He starts and stops the game clock and keeps the referee informed of the time remaining. He acts for the referee on downfield play.

THE BACK JUDGE

In professional football, the *back judge* takes over the responsibility of timing the game and checks for infractions in his side zone.

The use of a Back Judge is *optional* in College football, but is *required* in Professional.

THE SIDE JUDGE

The *side judge* has primary responsibility to make decisions involving the sideline of his side of the field, including catching, recovery, or illegal touching of a loose ball beyond the line of scrimmage; rules on plays involving pass receiver, including legality of catch or pass interference.

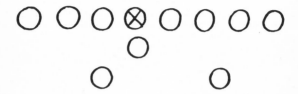

SCRIMMAGE LINE

Count the number of players on the scrimmage line. One man too many? Not at all. An *eight-man line* may be a very rare sight in football, but there is nothing in the rules to make it illegal. This is also true of a nine-man line or a ten-man line. What the rules do require is that there be *at least seven men* on the scrimmage line in order for the formation to be legal. Paul Brown, the former head coach of the Cleveland Browns, once invented and used plays based on an eight-man line.

ILLEGAL FORMATION

This five-man line is illegal under the rules since it does not meet the seven-man minimum required on the scrimmage line.

LEGAL LEG LOCK

It is legal for the two *guards* and the *center* to line up and *lock legs*. The rules permit this, but only for the center and the guards. It is against the rules for other linemen to lock legs. This unusual way for players to line up is not used today for tactical reasons, not because the rules forbid it.

NEUTRAL ZONE

Because one careless player (No. 68), has placed his hand too far forward, the team will draw an *offside* penalty. All linemen except the center are required to be behind their scrimmage line. Only the *center* is allowed to have any part of his body *in the neutral zone*. The neutral zone is measured by the *length of the football* and is the area between the offensive and defensive scrimmage lines. The center, however, is not permitted to be beyond the neutral zone. Should he place himself beyond the neutral zone, the team will draw an offside penalty.

MAN IN MOTION

As this backfield man (No. 23) goes into motion before the ball is snapped, all his teammates must remain stationary because only *one player* is allowed to be in motion. But he became careless as to the direction he is taking. He is moving toward the scrimmage line. In all cases, the man in motion should be traveling a path either parallel to or away from the scrimmage line. Otherwise, his team will be penalized 5 yards.

END IN MOTION

This looks like the start of the old-fashioned end-around play. The end (No. 83) appears to be legally in motion because he is traveling a path backward from the line of scrimmage as the ball is about to be snapped. But the formation is illegal because, having started from the scrimmage line, he has left only six players on the line. The rule requires at least seven linemen. The penalty is 5 yards. It is important to remember that in properly executing one maneuver that infractions of other rules are not committed.

RETURN BEFORE SNAP (Offensive)

An over-anxious lineman (No. 71) has "jumped" the signal and crossed the scrimmage line before the ball is snapped. He immediately recovers and returns to his set position, or three-point stance, without making contact with an opponent. The play still has not started but the lineman is declared to have made a false start. The rule is that once an offensive lineman has assumed a set position, he cannot charge or move in such a way as to lead an opposing player to think the ball is being snapped. The penalty is 5 yards.

RETURN BEFORE SNAP (Defensive)

The defensive lineman (No. 75) has charged into the neutral zone and then has returned to his proper position behind the defensive scrimmage line. Since the ball has not been snapped and no contact was made with an opponent, he is not considered to be offside and there is no penalty. However, if the defensive lineman does this repeatedly after having been warned, he will be penalized 5 yards.

OFFSETTING PENALTIES

If both the offensive and defensive linemen have charged before the ball is snapped, and the official rules that they did so *simultaneously,* then a double foul is called and the penalties offset each other. However, if it is ruled that the action of the offensive player caused his opponent to go offside, then the offensive team will be penalized 5 yards.

OFFSETTING PENALTIES

The defensive lineman charges into his opponent before the ball is snapped. At the same time the center lifts the football off the ground. While the defensive team will be ruled offside, the center will be penalized for an illegal snap because he is allowed only one *continuous* motion to pass the ball back. Thus the penalties will offset each other.

SNAPPING (CENTERING) THE BALL

Snapping (centering) the ball is the start of every play from scrimmage. If the center doesn't handle this part of the play properly, then the offensive team is in trouble. The center is expected not to raise either end of the ball more than 45 degrees before the snap. He must keep the football pointing toward the opponent's goal line. He must hand or pass the ball back in one continuous motion and is not permitted to fake a snap.

ADVANCING THE BALL

At any time, it is legal for the man with the ball (No. 28) to hand it backward or to pass it backward or to the side (lateral) to a teammate.

HANDING BALL FORWARD

The football may be handed forward from one back (No. 17) to another (No. 21) during scrimmage play, but only if *both backs* are *behind the scrimmage line*. If the backs are beyond the scrimmage line, such action is illegal.

HAND-OFF TO LINEMAN

The only occasion on which a lineman is allowed to receive a forward hand-off is illustrated by No. 67. He has turned around so that he faces his own goal line and is at least 1 yard behind the scrimmage line.

THE STIFF-ARM

The ball-carrier (or runner) is employing a standard technique — the stiff arm — to prevent an opponent from tackling him. The ball-carrier is permitted to use his hand or an arm to push away an opponent.

ILLEGAL HELP TO RUNNER

A teammate is trying to help the ball-carrier gain a few more yards. This is illegal and the team will receive a 15-yard penalty. Members of the offensive team are not allowed to push, lift or otherwise assist the runner directly.

BLOCKING

A legal shoulder block is being completed upon No. 79. The rule states that a blocker is not permitted to use his hands or arms.

This is the classic stance of a blocker who is keeping his hands in contact with his chest. He must also be sure to keep his hands and arms below the shoulders of the opponent he is blocking.

This blocking technique is illegal. The blocker has forgotten a cardinal rule by locking his hands together. He will be penalized 15 yards for the infraction.

31

ILLEGAL ARM INTERLOCK

There is strength in teamwork, but not in this case. Blockers are not permitted to interlock arms. The penalty for this type of blocking is 15 yards.

BODY BLOCK

The blocker is putting a body, or crab, block on his opponent (No. 76). In making this type of block, he is not required to keep his hand or arm in contact with his body.

USE OF HANDS

The offensive player (No. 77) is trying to push his opponent (No. 68) with his hands. Such action is in violation of the rule and is punished by a 15-yard penalty. *No blocker is allowed to use his hands to push, pull or grab an opposing player.*

The blocker (No. 88) is violating the rule forbidding the use of hands or arms to hook or clamp an opposing player (No. 69). He also cannot use his hands or arms to obstruct or interfere with an opposing player. The penalty for this infraction is 15 yards.

At first glance, this may appear to be an illegal block because the blocker (No. 78) has contacted his opponent above the shoulders. When the defensive player (No. 87), by trying to duck or submarine under the blocker, is responsible for the "high" block, no penalty is called against the blocker.

TACKLING

The defender (No. 7) is making the standard two-armed tackle to bring the runner (No. 17) down. As soon as any part of the runner's body, except his hands and feet, touches the ground, he is not permitted to make any further advance. In High School and College rules a runner is "down" whether he has touched the ground because of a tackle or simply through slipping or falling. In Professional football, when a runner slips or falls he is not considered "down" and may continue to advance the ball until he is tackled.

This may not be the classic way to make a tackle, but it is *legal to grab the runner* around the neck or any part of his body. The tackler, however, has to be sure that he is not grabbing the runner's face mask.

A push in time may stop a long gain and the defender (No. 88) is within the rules when he pushes the runner (No. 25) to the ground. The defense is allowed to use hands and arms to tackle, push, shove or otherwise *throw the runner* to the ground.

LEGAL USE OF HANDS

The defender (No. 78) is using his hands in a legal manner to push the blocker and pursue the runner. A *defensive player* is allowed to use his hands and arms to grasp, push, pull or lift other offensive players out of his way if he is trying to reach the runner.

DISQUALIFYING FOUL

The defensive player (No. 70) will be disqualified for *punching* his opponent (No. 15) and his team will be penalized 15 yards. The rule forbids any player from striking another with his fist, forearm, elbow or locked hands, or to kick or knee an opponent. The *disqualifying foul* rule differs from the *personal foul* rule in that the action is considered by the officials to be performed deliberately and willfully with intent to harm.

PERSONAL FOULS

KNEEING

The blocker (No. 76) is guilty of *kneeing* his opponent (No. 15) and is penalized 15 yards since it is not considered a deliberate act. Under the same rule no player shall hit an opponent either on the head, neck or face with the heel, back or side of the hand or with the wrist.

ACCIDENTAL KICK

No. 47 has *inadvertently kicked* an opposing player on the ground while trying to reach the runner. He will be penalized 15 yards under the rule that prohibits any player from swinging his foot and striking another player above the knee with his foot.

TRIPPING

The runner (No. 12) is being tripped by the defensive player (No. 17) and the infraction will cost the team on defense 15 yards *Tripping* is never allowed, regardless of whether the tripped player is carrying the ball or not.

PILING ON

Since the runner is already on the ground, the defensive player (No. 19) who is about to fall on him will be guilty of *piling on* and will be penalized 15 yards. Once the ball becomes dead players are expected to stop running into or throwing themselves on an opponent.

Any hurdling by the runner (No. 11) is best left for the track event. He will be penalized 15 yards for jumping over an opponent at the scrimmage line.

When the runner (No. 12) is obviously out of bounds, no defensive player may tackle him. The penalty is 15 yards.

CLIPPING

The block being performed on No. 69 is called *clipping* and, contrary to popular belief, it is *not necessarily illegal.* Clipping means a player has thrown himself across the back of the legs or the back of an opponent other than the runner. In a scrimmage play clipping is permitted in an area about 6 yards in depth and 4 yards wide on each side of the middle lineman. But any offensive player outside this area who is in motion toward the ball when it is snapped may not clip in this area. During a kick-off, or other free-kick down, no clipping is permitted. The penalty is 15 yards.

The referee has already taken possession of the ball, making it clear the play is over. The illegal tackle will draw a 15-yard penalty under the rule that bars any player from running into or making contact with an opponent obviously out of the play either before or after the ball is dead.

The face mask or protector is off-limits and grabbing a player's mask is forbidden. The penalty is 15 yards.

FORWARD PASS

ILLEGAL PASS

The passer (No. 21) has gone one step too far before throwing the ball because his left foot has *crossed the neutral zone*. It is is 5 yards from the spot of the pass and the down counts.

LEGAL PASS

The passer is now able to throw the ball legally even though he has stepped past his own scrimmage line. He has been careful not to go beyond the neutral zone.

INTENTIONAL GROUNDING

The passer will be penalized for throwing the ball away to prevent loss of yardage. He is about to be tackled and brought down. Since there is no receiver reasonably near the area, the passer is guilty of *intentionally grounding the pass*. The penalty is loss of 15 yards and a down.

JUDGMENT CALL

This passing situation is more complicated. The passer, No. 11, throws the ball in the general direction of the receiver just as he is about to be tackled. The question that the referee has to settle is whether it was a bona-fide attempt at completing a pass or whether it was a clever attempt to prevent a loss on the play. This is a judgment call and, unless the evidence is overwhelming on the other side, the official will rule it a legal forward pass.

ELIGIBLE RECEIVERS

The arrows point to the only players on the offensive team who are eligible pass receivers: the two ends on the scrimmage line and the players in the backfield who are at least 1 yard in back of the scrimmage line. In Professional football, the T quarterback is not an eligible receiver. The rule on eligible receivers remains the same regardless of whether the end man is a tackle or guard in another formation. All 11 players on the defensive team are eligible to intercept a pass.

STEPPING OUT-OF-BOUNDS

In the illustration at the left, an otherwise eligible receiver has made himself ineligible by going out-of-bounds before returning to the field to catch a pass. On the right, the ineligible receiver becomes eligible because the pass has been touched by a defensive player.

LANDING OUT-OF-BOUNDS

The receiver, No. 21, made a nice catch of the forward pass, but the effort was wasted. Though he is inbounds when he leaped for the ball, he landed outside the sideline. In such a situation the receiver is ruled out-of-bounds and the pass is incomplete.

PRETENDED FUMBLE

The runner, No. 19, is attempting to execute a clever maneuver by throwing the ball forward, pretending to fumble so that teammate No. 77 will recover the ball for additional yardage. But any attempt to throw the ball forward beyond the neutral zone is classified as an illegal forward pass and will be penalized 5 yards from that point.

SIMULTANEOUS CATCH

In this example "half a loaf" is about as good as a whole one. The intended receiver (No. 89) and the defender (No. 21) caught the pass simultaneously. It will be ruled a completed pass and the ball given to the passing team. There is a limitation in such a situation: the receiver may not advance the ball.

TOUCHING INELIGIBLE RECEIVER

The passing team may appear to be lucky because the football has bounced off the helmet of one of its players (No. 68) into the hands of another. But it will not be ruled a completed forward pass because the ball, even if only accidentally, touched an ineligible receiver first.

JUDGMENT CALL

The receiver caught the forward pass, or did he? He has possession of the ball momentarily. It slipped through his hands just as he was about to take his first step. *The judgment of the nearest official* will determine whether the receiver actually had possession of the ball or whether the ruling should be an incomplete pass.

PLAYING THE BALL

Appearances can be deceiving. It ma seem as if the defender (No. 12) is interferi with the receiver's right to catch the forwar pass but it is not pass interference. Eligib players on both teams have equal rights to th football so long as they are making a legi mate attempt to catch it, or, as it is oft called, *"playing the ball"* rather than the o ponent. Any contact that ensues as a result legal.

PASS INTERFERENCE

This is pass interference even though the offender (No. 17) has not made contact with the receiver (No. 88). No. 17 is attempting to distract the receiver from catching the pass by waving his arms in front of him. With his back to the play, the defender is not making an honest effort to "play the ball." Under the rule it is the passing team's ball at the spot of the foul.

BEFORE THE PASS IS THROWN

The defender (No. 17) is not guilty of pass interference because contact with the receiver (No. 89) was made before the ball was thrown and was beyond the scrimmage line.

INELIGIBLE RECEIVER DOWNFIELD

Offensive guard (No. 69), having completed his primary block on the opposing defensive player, is running downfield to assist with the blocking for the intended receiver. He is, however, committing an infraction of the rules: once he has lost contact with his opponent he cannot make a move downfield until the pass is thrown. He is not an eligible receiver and should not be downfield. The team will be penalized 10 yards for having an ineligible receiver downfield.

PASS INTERFERENCE RULE

Even though the pass thrown by No. 17 has not yet crossed the scrimmage line, pass interference rules are in effect. The rules apply from *the moment the pass is thrown*. The defensive player (No. 25) is guilty of interfering with the intended pass receiver (No. 89) and the penalty will give the passing team a first down at the spot where the interference occurred.

ALMOST A SAFETY

The defensive player (No. 78) has almost scored 2 points for his team by batting back a forward pass thrown from the end zone. If he had been *inside the end zone* instead of a few yards out when he batted back the pass, he would have been credited with a safety.

DEAD BALL

The *ball is ruled dead* the instant a forward pass hits a goal post, even though it may bounce off and be caught by a player before it touches the ground. The rules state that the ball is dead upon hitting the goal posts, the crossbar, the ground or going out of bounds.

FUMBLE ON A PASS PLAY

The passer (No. 12) has fumbled the ball in attempting to pass it forward to an eligible receiver (No. 27) behind the scrimmage line. It is ruled a fumble and not an incomplete pass. The importance of this is that now the defensive team can recover the ball. If it were an incomplete pass the passing team would automatically retain possession of the ball.

INTERCEPTION

The pass has touched an ineligible receiver and the defender (No. 89) is about to intercept. The ruling is that *the interception stands* unless the defensive team prefers to take the penalty. A forward pass remains in play *only for an interception after touching an ineligible receiver*. In Professional football there is a penalty for intentional touching, none for accidental.

SCHOOL AND PRO RULE

Two *eligible receivers* have caught the pass simultaneously. In High School and College it is ruled a completed pass, but among the Professionals it is ruled incomplete.

BATTING BALL ON A PASS PLAY

The defender (No. 21) bats the attempted forward pass away from the intended receiver (No. 27). Under the rule the *defense* is allowed to bat the pass in any direction and at any time but the *offense* is allowed only to bat the ball to prevent an interception.

KICKING

KICK-OFF FORMATION

Five players of the *team receiving* the kick-off must be in an area 10 to 15 yards from the kick-off, between the 50-yard line and their own 45-yard line. There are no restrictions on where the other players are located, except that they must be in back of the first five players.

Note: In the NFL, the kick-off is made from the 35-yard line.

56

FREE-KICK FORMATION

The free kick follows a safety. Five players of the *team receiving* the kick must be in an area 10 to 15 yards from the ball, between the 30-yard line and the 35-yard line.

KICK-OFF

The ball is put into play at the start of each half by the *kick-off*. The ball is placed on the 40-yard line of the kicking team, usually resting on a tee, but a place-kick or a drop-kick may be used legally. The kick-off is also used to put the ball in play after a field goal or try-for-point after a touchdown.

PUNT

The punt is usually used on a scrimmage play. The ball is kicked before it touches the ground. It may also be used as a free-kick after a safety. Team punting gives up possession of the ball.

58

PLACE-KICK

The ball is held for the kicker by a teammate. The place-kick is used to score a field-goal, point-after-touchdown, and sometimes on a kick-off.

DROP-KICK

The kicker drops the ball and kicks it just at the instant it touches the ground or a fraction of a second later. Seldom employed today, it can be used instead of the place-kick.

ILLEGALLY KICKING THE BALL

The ball may not be kicked by any player except during a specific kicking play. Since the defensive player (No. 12) has deliberately kicked a free ball, the offensive team has possession of the ball at the spot where the rule infraction occurred. If the player on offense kicks the ball, his team is given a 15-yard penalty from the starting point of the play.

ROUGHING THE KICKER

After the punter (No. 27) kicks the ball, an opposing player crashes into him: a clear violation of roughing-the-kicker regulations. The purpose of the rule is to protect the kicker and the holder of a place-kick during a scrimmage kick because they are vulnerable to contact. To gain protection under the rules, it has to be reasonably obvious that a kick will be made. Penalty for roughing the kicker is 15 yards.

ON A BLOCKED PUNT

A roughing-the-kicker penalty will not be called on this play because *the punt has been blocked*. Such contact is considered a legitimate play when the punt is blocked. The defensive player (No. 77), therefore, is not violating any rules by running into the kicker.

SLIGHT CONTACT

When the contact is slight, the defensive player (No. 77) will not be called for roughing the kicker.

ON THE QUICK KICK

Since a *quick kick* was attempted, the defensive player (No. 70) is exempt from the roughing-the-kicker rule because it was not reasonably obvious that a scrimmage kick was planned. No penalty.

FUMBLE ON KICKING PLAY A fumble before the kick is attempted also exem the defensive players from the roughing-the-kicker rule.

FAIR CATCH

WRONG   **RIGHT**

FAIR CATCH SIGNAL

If the signal for a *fair catch* is given improperly, the receiving team is penalized 5 yards from the spot of the foul. On the left, the wrong way to signal; on the right, the player gives the proper signal.

PROTECTING PUNT RECEIVER

The players crowd about the man catching the ball but they have to be careful to give him an *unmolested opportunity* to catch it. If they interfere, the penalty is 15 yards.

ILLEGAL INTERFERENCE ON A CATCH

Even though he manages to catch the ball as he is being tackled, his team will be awarded a 15-yard penalty. Under the rule, illegal interference is called when a player is tackled before or when the ball arrives.

NO FUMBLE ON CATCH

Although the receiver of the punt fumbled while he was being tackled, the official will rule no fumble. His opponent will be penalized 15 yards. The receiving team will retain possession of the ball because of the illegal interference.

FAIR TACKLE

The receiver of the punt has fumbled and then is tackled by an opponent. No interference will be called. Protection against interference with the opportunity to catch a kick ends when the player *touches the ball*, except when it is a fair catch.

TWO-STEP LIMIT

After making a fair catch, a player is allowed to take only two steps. The ball becomes dead at the spot where he caught it. If he tries to advance, he will be penalized 5 yards.

OFFICIAL'S CODE OF SIGNALS

OFFSIDE. A player on either team has crossed his scrimmage line before the ball has been snapped (put into play). Penalty: 5 yards.

ILLEGAL RETURN. Return of a substitute previously disqualified, or before a down has been completed (College). Penalty: 15 yards.

ILLEGAL PROCEDURE. This indicates several different infractions, the more common being: false start; having less than 7 players on the offensive team's scrimmage line; illegally handing the ball forward; taking more than 2 steps after a fair catch; illegal snap; infraction of substitution rules (College); invalid fair-catch signal (Professional).

DELAY OF GAME. Excess time-outs requested or used; illegal delay of game; crawling (High School and College); team not ready to play (College penalty: 15 yards); illegal substitution (High School); interference with opponent or snap of the ball (High School). Penalty: 5 yards.

ILLEGAL MOTION. Player or players illegally in motion when the ball is snapped. Penalty: 5 yards.

PERSONAL FOUL. Piling on; hurdling; tripping; tackling out-of-bounds; running into opponent obviously out of play; striking; kicking or kneeing an opponent; tackling player who signalled for fair catch; grabbing the face mask of opponent (College). Penalty: 5 yards.

ILLEGAL SHIFT. Player or players failed to stop for one second after a shift. Penalty: 5 yards.

PERSONAL FOUL. In Professional football, the referee will give an additional signal to define more precisely the rule infraction.

INTENTIONAL GROUNDING OF PASS. Penalty: 15 yards and loss of down.

CLIPPING. A foul committed when a player attempts to block from behind by throwing himself across the back or legs of an opposing player other than the runner. Penalty: 15 yards.

ILLEGALLY PASSING OR HANDING THE BALL FORWARD. Penalty: 5 yards and loss of down.

ROUGHING-THE-KICKER. The kicker, or the holder of the ball for the place-kick, has been run into or otherwise illegally interfered with. Penalty: 15 yards.

PASS OR KICK INTERFERENCE. Offensive pass interference: 10-yard penalty. Defensive pass interference: Pass ruled completed at spot of foul. Interference with fair-catch opportunity: 15-yard penalty.

UNSPORTSMANLIKE CONDUCT. Besides general unsportsmanlike conduct by player or coach, the signal also indicates: persons illegally on the field; delaying start of either half (High School); invalid signal for a fair catch (College). Penalty: 15 yards.

ILLEGAL RECEIVER DOWNFIELD. Penalty: 10 yards.

ILLEGAL USE OF HANDS. Penalty: 15 yards.

ILLEGALLY KICKING, BATTING, OR TOUCHING BALL. Illegal kick: 5-yard penalty; illegally kicking ball: 15-yard penalty; illegally kicking or batting free ball: College rules give the offended team possession of the ball at the spot where foul was committed; High School rules call for a 15-yard penalty; forward pass illegally touched: College rules provide for 5 or 15 yards penalty and/or loss of down.

INCOMPLETE FORWARD PASS. The signal also indicates a penalty has been refused; a field-goal or point-after-touchdown kick has been missed.

TIME-OUT. In High School and College games, if the official calls for time-out on his own, he taps his chest; in Professional football, the official places one hand on his cap.

INTERLOCKED INTERFERENCE, OR HELPING THE RUNNER. Penalty: 15 yards. In Professional football only, crawling: 5-yard penalty.

FIRST DOWN. The team in possession of the ball has a first down and now has four downs (plays) in which to gain 10 yards for another first down.

BALL IS DEAD.

SCORE. Touchdown, field goal, or place-kick has been made.

BALL IS READY FOR PLAY.

SAFETY.

GAME CLOCK STARTS.